Be Happy and Forgive!

Eliminate Negative Thinking, Let Go the Past and Find Joy in Every Day – A Mind Breaking Self Help Guide on Happiness with new Scientific Insights | Mindfulness Gift

SARAH P. BALDWIN

ISBN - 9798784688590

Contents

The science of negative thoughts

CHAPTER 5

Making the choice to forgive and surrender attachments

Introduction

The past. It's something that whether we like it or not, we spend a lot of time thinking about. Our past experiences and actions come to define who we are as we go about our lives but can also be something that we hold onto and find impossible to let go of.

There's a famous quote from Buddha, which has formed the basis of this book you'll be reading: *"Do not dwell in the past, do not dream of the future, concentrate the mind on the present moment."*

Many of us may find ourselves looking back on our past, evaluating the choices and decisions we made. Maybe this leaves you feeling disappointed, regretful, or negative. These feelings could be directed towards the person we were, or the way that we continue to hold onto feelings about how people treated us.

Dwelling on the past too much can often rob us of time spent enjoying the present, the most important moment. The here and now. Learning to focus our minds on what we're experiencing—as we're experiencing them—is one of the greatest skills that we can develop.

You are not your past

Although the past has made you who you are in this moment, don't forget that the person you were in the past is not the person that you are now. Change is part of life that we can't avoid. Of course, you should look back and reflect on yourself, but it's also important to learn to separate the person you were and the person that you have become.

In this book, you will learn the ways to identify when negative thoughts are holding you back and how you can avoid them entering your brain in the first place. We are going to give ourselves the freedom to let go of the past, to let go of previous emotions, pain, and hurt.

You're allowed to move on, you're allowed to heal.

Your past will always be a part of you, of course, but reliving habits and going through the motions of past experiences is not a way that you can live your life.

Life is a journey, one where every day we take one step towards our goals. If your goal is to combat negative thoughts, it won't happen overnight. It's going to be a case of taking small steps to change your life and ways of thinking.

Think about your baggage

People use the term 'baggage' a lot when it comes to the past. As we go through our lives, we of course all pick up this baggage—this might be emotional baggage in the form of trauma, negative or positive experiences, and encounters with other people, or physical baggage like people, and physical objects.

Although the term baggage tends to connote something negative, it may not always be this way. Your baggage may be the thing that's making you stronger, providing for you in your journey through life. However, sometimes this baggage may feel like a huge rock that you're carrying on your back.

When you feel the weight of your past on your shoulders making you think that you can't go any further, it's time for you to take a break and be with your emotions. Think about how you feel and come up with a plan to alleviate some of the stress that you've been holding.

Take stock of your baggage, what is it that you're taking forward with you? Do you want to take this on your journey with you? Or can you leave it behind?

Be happy and forgive!

This book will act as a guide to anyone who feels the past hanging over them and affecting them every day.

Is it possible that we've been approaching our feelings the wrong way this whole time? Have you been trying to ignore them and move on, rather than facing them head-on and refusing to give them power?

Do any of these situations apply to you?

- ☐ I'm struggling to forgive someone for how they treated me

- ☐ I feel demotivated in my everyday life

- ☐ When I think about the past, I feel regret and disappointment

- ☐ My past has a negative affect on how I live my life now

- ☐ I can't let go of someone from my past

- ☐ My past destructive habits have continued to follow me throughout life

If you resonate with any of these points of views, this book is for you.

This book is not going to be telling you how to feel, or simply explaining why you feel the way that you do. Instead, this book will delve deep into why our brains work the way they do and why we often struggle to live in the present.

In this book, you will find actionable tips, activities, and guides on the small, everyday habits that you can easily incorporate into your life to make a big difference in your happiness.

Your problems won't be solved the second you close this book, but it will be a starting point for your healing journey. You will feel equipped with the knowledge, and resources, you need to make a positive difference in your life.

Imagine a life, a few weeks, months, or years from now. A life where you feel at peace, you feel like you truly live in the moment and find joy in the things that you may have once thought mundane and boring. A life where you feel genuinely happy, you don't ask for more and you don't feel like you're missing out.

You also don't feel the dark shadows of your past looming behind your every step or trying to push their weight on to your shoulders.

This book does not promise all the answers, nor does it offer a quick fix that will solve everyone's problems. This book provides a plan of action, a nudge in the right direction based on personal experience and scientific insights.

We hope that this guide becomes the first step on your healing journey that can transform your life to make you happier, at peace and free of negative thoughts.

How does the past define you?

The past is something that none of us can escape, it can sometimes be the catalyst for us achieving a brighter, more fulfilled future, but it can also be the thing that holds us back from achieving our full potential.

Our outlook on life, the way we look at the world and the feelings we have about ourselves changes over time— sometimes for the better, but it can also be for the worst.

If you have behaved a certain way in the past, it's likely that you will continue to repeat this behavior in your present and future[1] without even being aware of it. But it also comes down to how you perceive your past behavior that can seriously impact your current reality[2].

---

1 Ouellette JA, Wood W. Habit and intention in everyday life: The multiple processes by which past behavior predicts future behavior. Psychological Bulletin. 1998;124:54–74.

2 Albarracín D, Wyer RS Jr. The cognitive impact of past behavior: influences on beliefs, attitudes, and future behavioral decisions. J Pers Soc Psychol. 2000;79(1):5-22. doi:10.1037//0022-3514.79.1.5

When we spend too much of our time focusing on the past and not allowing ourselves the freedom to enjoy the present, we limit ourselves to our old habits and ways of doing things. These previous actions come to define our present reality, rather than allowing us to grow and evolve every day.

Paying attention to how we were in the past is important, it can help us identify and evaluate certain behaviors and how they serve us. But if you dwell on these previous events and feelings too much, you trap yourself in a place of constant negativity.

How much does your past affect you?

We're all a culmination of our past. The person we are today has been influenced by a variety of factors; how we were brought up by our parents, the school we attended, our relationships with our friends, our romantic relationships and even the government style of the country we were born in.

Are you unhappy with the person you are now and the future that you can envisage because of how things were in the past?

Many people across the world are living their daily lives hanging onto the burdens of the mistakes and decisions they made in the past.

Sometimes you may feel fine, that you're happy and motivated. But often, all it takes is the smallest reminder of the past and you're instantly taken back to your old habits and decision-making processes that hold no value in your present life.

The inability to let yourself be defined by your present leads you towards negative thinking, a lack of happiness and being unable to move forward in life.

However troubled your past may have been, you don't have to sit around, wishing that you can make a difference and change your life.

Happiness doesn't happen overnight and letting go of important moments in your past can also not be automatically wiped from your brain, but you can learn to readjust your perspectives and find alternative methods to cope with the pain and negative thoughts of your past.

It's OK that sometimes your past negative choices outweigh the positive ones that you're making in the present.

It's also OK to wish that you could go back in time and change the decisions you made but unfortunately this will never be possible, and you must learn to live with this fact.

Look after yourself and your mind, stop letting these negative thoughts intrude where they are not wanted and build a much better, and more positive, life for yourself.

The psychology of your past

There is a science for why you may be left feeling that you can't let go of the past, and it all comes down to psychology and the way that the brain works.

Our behavior is the result of personality and motivational factors that have developed through experiences in our lives[3]. For example, if you once went for a job interview and it didn't go so well, you may be left with negative thoughts about going for another one. This is a dangerous negative thought as the security of having a job that you enjoy is extremely important for our social wellbeing.

The way that our past self behaved in certain situations is usually remembered by the brain, therefore we continue to act the same if these situations repeat themselves[4]. Your brain may not be able to tell that our previous actions resulted in a negative situation, so we repeat ourselves. We go through the motions of our past repeatedly and then are left wondering why the negative outcomes always remain the same.

---

3 Eagly AH, Chaiken S. The psychology of attitudes. San Diego, CA: Harcourt Brace; 1993

4 Taylor SE. On inferring one's attitudes from one's behavior: Some delimiting conditions. Journal of Personality and Social Psychology. 1975;31:126–131.

Normally, if an outcome of a situation was not positive, the brain will avoid making the same mistake again[5], but this may not be the case every time.

There is a theory about dissonance reduction[6] that says when people realize that they have voluntarily performed a behavior that contradicts the normal response, they try and rationalize their behavior. This is often the case when it comes to negative behavioral traits.

When you act in a certain way that does not provide you with your preferred outcome, you may try to rationalize it in your mind. This means that you convince yourself that it was right, rather than owning up to the fact that it did not serve you. This way of thinking is what will continue to keep you stuck in the past and limited from moving forward.

5 Skinner BF. Science and human behavior. New York: Macmillan; 1953.

6 Festinger L. A theory of cognitive dissonance. Evanston, IL: Row, Peterson; 1957.

CHAPTER 1 ACTIVITY

Answer the following questions. Before writing down your answers, take time to think about your feelings and emotions and then allow yourself to write.

1. Describe the person you were 5 years ago

_____

_____

_____

2. How close do you feel to this person?

_____

_____

_____

3. What did you worry about 5 years ago?

_____

_____

_____

4. If you spoke to the person you were 5 years ago now, how would you feel?

_____

_____

_____

5. Where did you think you would be in 5 years' time?

_____

_____

_____

Simple ways to redefine your views on the past

No matter what you do, there's no way to completely get rid of your past. You simply won't be able to erase all memory of the person you were and the decisions that you made.

After all, we are all like a puzzle, with our past creating the pieces being put in place to make the finished product. If even one piece of this puzzle is missing, we can never be complete.

You can spend your time trying to forget everything, but we assure you that this tactic will never work in the long term.

Identify your habit loops

Our brain works in loops, when we have habits and routines there is a reason why we make them repeatedly. This cycle of repetition can be described as a habit loop.

TRIGGER – ROUTINE – OUTCOME

This is how our feelings of the past seem to rear their heads repeatedly, and the reason why we can't seem to change the outcome.

Identifying these habit loops are the first step in redefining your views on the past.

1. Trigger

There are many things in our daily lives that can trigger us and take us back to our past. This could be as simple as finding yourself in the same situation again, or even performing a similar action or saying a triggering word.

Triggers are different for everyone but can have disastrous effect. These triggers are the reason why your negative feelings come out to play so often.

Think about times when negative thoughts and feelings have impacted you recently. What was the trigger of these feelings?

If you can start to notice your triggers and the things that cause negative behavior—like a person, place or object—you're one step closer to breaking this loop and freeing yourself from the past.

2. Routine

After this trigger has affected you, you'll find yourself falling back into an already planned routine. This is the point in the loop where you start to behave in the same way you did in the past.

These actions could be you thinking negative thoughts, engaging in behavior that you *know* is not going to result in a good outcome for you, or falling back into relationships and remembering the grudges you felt for someone or something.

Routines can be hard to break, but not impossible. Think about the routines you adopt and notice how they affect you.

3. Outcome

After the routine, you get the outcome. Normally if you have fallen foul to negative routines, this outcome is not going to be favorable or positive for you.

If you perform the same routines, you can never hope for a different outcome—it's always going to be the same.

If you find yourself in the routine of the same outcomes, think about the outcome. What has happened, why don't you want this, what would your preferred outcome be?

Now you've got a better understanding of your habit loops—which will help you to create actionable and effective routes to free you of negative thinking—it's time to work on redefining your outlook of life, we'll guide you with some points to consider.

Being realistic and thoughtful about the following points will help you to look at the past in a whole new light.

Why does the past matter?

Don't ignore the past but be critical when it comes to thinking about why the past matters to you.

Everyone's past is important to them. The past is not all bad, there are many positive things that have happened in everyone's life.

Rather than looking at the past as something that limits you, think of it as something valuable that you can look back at to draw on your previous experiences.

Memories can be lies

Not everything that you tell yourself about the past is true, sometimes we remember situations differently, or avoid certain details so that we don't get the full picture.

For example, think of the most embarrassing situation in your life when you were around other people. In your memory you remember it as everyone laughing at you, feeling insecure and ashamed of yourself. But some of the people there may not have noticed what happened or may not have thought it was that embarrassing at all—it's only your brain that has convinced you to be embarrassed.

The past is the present

You should stop thinking of the past as this far away thing that's haunting you, instead you must realize the past is the present. The present slips away from us so quickly that everything turns into the past within seconds.

The way to deal with your past and change it is to live your present in a positive, happy way and before you know it, this present is now your past.

You're the editor

Although you may not feel like it, you're the editor of your own life. It's up to you alone how you deal with situations and how you grow as a person.

Once you realize the power that you hold, you will start to realize that you can change your thinking and behavior.

Question yourself

Don't sit back and let yourself think about the past in a certain way, constantly question yourself.

☐   Why do I feel this way about the past?

☐   Is what I'm telling myself about the past true?

☐   Are my views of the past helping me right now?

CHAPTER 2 ACTIVITY

Below, you'll find a Venn diagram for you to fill in, or you could draw your own in a notebook.

On the left-hand side of the diagram, fill in all the things you know about the habits, behaviors, and feelings that you followed in the past. On the right-hand side, fill in all the same information but for how you are in the future.

In the middle you can put all the things that have remained the same. These are the things that you are holding onto in your current reality. Once you have identified these things, we can start to evaluate whether these are positive or negative things, and if they are the triggers that are holding you back from being happy and finding the joy in every day.

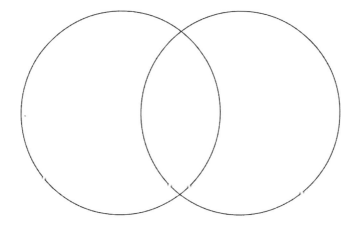

CHAPTER 3

Can you identify your own self-sabotaging behavior?

In the past chapters, we worked on the past and coming to terms with what how it plays a part in the person we've become in the present.

We've tried to redefine our views on the past, rather than dwelling on it, we should be using it to better ourselves and learn how to let it go to be a better version of ourselves.

Now it's time to think about your actions in your present that are the immediate causes of your negative thinking.

We are going to be calling this self-sabotaging behavior, this is behavior where you get in your own way, hold yourself back and stop yourself from being happy.

There are many causes for self-sabotaging behavior and holding onto the past is one of the main ones that many people face.

The first step to working on these behaviors and eliminating them from your life is to identify when they occur.

Self-sabotaging can sometimes be the easy option when you're trying to meet an important goal. You know that you want to work towards this goal, but rather than motivating yourself to reach it, you act in a way that directly stops you from doing it.

A great example is when students want to get a good grade on a paper. They know that in order to do this they have to be disciplined and go to the library to work, but because this requires a lot of effort, they take the easy option of going out with their friends or procrastinating at home.

This behavior directly stops them from being able to write their paper, meaning that in the end they must rush their work and find it impossible to get the grade that they were hoping for.

Another example is when you are holding a grudge over someone in your past. The harder option is to see them, talk through the issues and try and come to a resolution. You know that this is something that you need to do to move on from a potentially hard situation, but you also know that it could raise tension or awkwardness. Instead, you go for the easier option of continuing to hold the grudge. This directly stops you from being able to move on from your feelings and keeps you in a constant loop of negative thoughts.

With self-sabotaging behavior, there are normally 2 forms that many people experience:

Conscious self-sabotage

Conscious self-sabotage is when you *know* that you are sabotaging yourself through your actions, but you do them anyway.

This is like the student procrastinating writing their paper. They understand that their behavior is going to get in the way of achieving their academic goals, but they choose to do it anyway.

This type of self-sabotage can be easier to solve as you're completely in control of your thoughts and feelings, it's just a case of breaking the negative habit.

Unconscious self-sabotage

Unconscious self-sabotage is the opposite, it's where you get in your own way but aren't aware of the impacts of what you're doing.

This form of self-sabotage usually develops over a period and is your mind's response to negative situations.

For example, if someone has a strong fear of being rejected by a romantic partner. They may start to unconsciously stop putting themselves in situations where rejection is possible, like suggesting a date, or communicating their needs. This stops them from experiencing rejection but is also going to be holding them back from having a fulfilling relationship with someone else.

Because these habits are often caused by trauma or experience, it can sometimes be harder to let go of, but with time and patience—and knowing when the self-sabotage is happening—you can easily break free from these actions.

Examples of self-sabotage

It can often be hard to identify when we are sabotaging ourselves, especially when we think that it's just the way that we work.

Here are some common examples of self-sabotaging behavior. Do any of these apply to you?

- ☐ Procrastination

- ☐ Lateness

- ☐ Commitment and intimacy issues

- ☐ 'Ghosting' or ignoring people who care about you

- ☐ Stress eating, drinking or substance abuse

- ☐ Over-analyzing situations and worrying

This is not an exhaustive list and is often not something you need to particularly worry about if you do these things from time-to-time. It's normal for everyone to procrastinate or worry about some things, but if you find yourself doing any of these very often to the detriment of your happiness, you may want to figure out a way to stop yourself from doing this.

CHAPTER 3 ACTIVITY

Here's an activity to help with identifying and solving your self-sabotaging habits.

1. I self-sabotage because... *(Pointers: What do you think you gain from self-sabotage? Why is self-sabotage the easy option for you?)*

   _____

   _____

   _____

2. When I self-sabotage I... *(Pointers: What is the usual outcome of your self-sabotaging actions? How do you feel after self-sabotaging?)*

   _____

   _____

   _____

3. Instead of self-sabotaging I could... *(Pointers: What are some alternative behaviors that you could adopt instead?)*

_____

_____

_____

4. Some opportunities in the future for self-sabotage are... *(Pointers: Are there any events coming up that could provide an opportunity for self-sabotage? A date, interview, meeting etc.)*

_____

_____

_____

5. If this situation arises, I will... *(Pointers: If the situation described in the previous question arises, how are you going to respond? Come up with some manifestations and mantras that can help)*

_____

_____

_____

CHAPTER 4

The science of negative thoughts

If you struggle with negative thoughts daily that leave you unable to find the joy in the every day, know that you're not alone.

In fact, there's a lot of psychological research that goes to show that we are all in fact hard-wired to think negatively as a default—it's something known as negative bias. According to negative bias, negative thoughts are often stronger than positive thoughts. Our brains hold on to negative thoughts for much longer, which is the reason it seems that we always seem to dwell on bad experiences for so long after they happen.

To put it scientifically, humans perceive negative situations to be more complex than positive ones. Therefore, we form complex cognitive representations of these situations that take up more of our attention and cognitive processing energy[7], which is why they constantly seem to be taking up so much of our thoughts.

---

7 Fiske ST. Attention and weight in person perception: The impact of negative and extreme behavior. Journal of Personality and Social Psychology. 1980;38:889–906.

How you develop beliefs about yourself

Throughout our lives, we develop beliefs and assumptions about our abilities[8] based on how we respond to different situations, how we perform tasks and the people that we surround ourselves with.

These beliefs that we have about ourselves are the main motivators for how we behave and approach life[9]. If these beliefs that we have about ourselves are negative; for example, we don't think we respond well to other people, we believe we always make the wrong decisions, or are surrounded by people who don't fulfill us, it causes us to behave in an overall negative manner.

If we believe that we are lacking in the ability to be happy, or to move on from harmful situations, it will directly affect our ambition[10]. These negative beliefs can skew our perception and interpretation of events and feedback[11]

8 Bem, D. J. An experimental analysis of self-persuasion. J. Exp. Soc. Psychol. 1, 199–218 (1965).

9 Bandura, A. Social cognitive theory: An agentic perspective. Annu. Rev. Psychol. 52, 1–26 (2001).

10 Bandura, A., Barbaranelli, C., Caprara, G. V. & Pastorelli, C. Self-efficacy beliefs as shapers of children's aspirations and career trajectories. Child Dev. 72, 187–206 (2001).

11 Blascovich, J. & McFarlin, D. B. Effects of self-esteem and per-formance feedback on future affective preferences and cognitive expectations. J. Pers. Soc. Psychol. 40, 521–531 (1981).

making us confirm these negative beliefs, which then controls our future behavior[12].

How negative thoughts affect us

The occasional negative thought is completely normal, after all it's impossible to be positive about everything all the time—especially when you find yourself in particularly tricky circumstances.

But if you find that you are constantly thinking negatively about everything, you must acknowledge how big of an impact this is having on your everyday life and take steps to change this.

Negative thoughts can lead to us feeling demotivated or avoiding certain situations that we know would benefit us which causes us to be in a never-ending cycle of negative self-related thoughts[13].

---

12 Kluger, A. N. & DeNisi, A. Effects of feedback intervention on performance: A historical review, a meta-analysis, and a preliminary feedback intervention theory. Psychol. Bull. 119, 254–284 (1996).

13 Heimberg, R. G., Brozovich, F. A. & Rapee, R. M. A cognitive-behavioral model of social anxiety disorder: Update and extension. In Social anxiety: Clinical, developmental, and social perspectives (eds Hofmann, S. G. & DiBartolo, P. M.) 395–422 (NY: Elsevier, 2010).

Not only do negative thoughts keep us in a spiral, but it can also even increase the risk of us developing mental health problems like anxiety and depression[14].

If you are constantly finding yourself putting a negative spin on everything that happens in your life, chances are that you also find yourself feeling more stressed, impatient, and angry, which are no ways that you should be living your life. You're altering your reality to something that is not true, yet constantly convincing yourself that it is.

How to take control of your negative thoughts

None of us wants to feel negative all the time, so the next time you find yourself in a negative mood where you can't seem to find the positive in the situation, think about these following points.

Call yourself out

Are you able to notice when your negative thoughts are getting the better of you? It may be that you're in a situation where you're supposed to feel happy or relieved, but instead you're feeling anxious and downbeat.

---

14 Kinderman P, Schwannauer M, Pontin E, Tai S. Psychological Processes Mediate the Impact of Familial Risk, Social Circumstances and Life Events on Mental Health. PLoS ONE. 2013;8(10).

When you find yourself doing this, call yourself out. Identify these emotions and don't let them continue.

Thoughts are not reality

Just because your brain is thinking them, doesn't mean these thoughts are true. It can be easy to worry and panic when you're in difficult circumstances, but that doesn't mean you have to be hard on yourself.

For example, you think you're bad at your job and you constantly tell yourself so. These thoughts are not reality. What are these thoughts based off? Has anyone at work told you that you're bad at your job? Probably not. You have no reason to think that you're bad at your job, and probably in reality everyone you work with probably thinks you're great at your job.

What would your friends/family do?

A lot of the time the negative thoughts that we have in our heads are ones that we wouldn't say in front of a close friend or family member—why is that? Because they're not rational.

When you have a negative thought, think about what a loved one would say if they knew you were feeling this way. Would they comfort you, tell you that you're wrong, or prove to you that your feelings aren't real?

Put a timer on it

As we've said, everyone has negative thoughts and perhaps something happened to you that really doesn't make you feel good. In these situations, it's OK to let your feelings out and be negative but put a timer on it. Let yourself be negative for an hour and then snap out of it.

Say it or write it down

Sometimes it takes writing a thought down, or saying it aloud, for you to see—or hear—it as it really is. Look at what you've written down or repeat your thoughts aloud again.

You may find that you say it aloud and realize just how silly you sound and get a good laugh out of it.

Replace the negative with a positive

For every negative thought or feeling, there's an equally positive alternative that you should be focusing on. It can be hard to turn a negative thought on its head and make it positive, but we promise that it's possible.

You can find out how to do this in any situation by completing the activity at the end of this chapter.

CHAPTER 4 ACTIVITY

Think of some of the negative thoughts that you have had today and write them in the left-hand column of the table below.

Now go through each thought and come up with a positive spin on it, to show that for every negative thought you have, there is in fact a positive way you can look at it.

Negative thoughts	Positive thoughts
• Example: I don't want to go to work today because I'm bad at my job.	• Example: I'm looking forward to going to work today as I'm still learning and improving every day.

CHAPTER 5

Making the choice to forgive and surrender attachments

When someone has done something that causes you deep pain and hurt, you often think that there's nothing that they could ever do that would make you forgive them—especially if they've done something that has really betrayed your trust in them.

In situations when someone hurts you, you will probably find yourself going through the following stages:

1. Shock

2. Anger

3. Grief

4. Healing

You start by feeling shocked. You don't understand why they did what they did to you, you don't understand why they would want to hurt you.

These feelings quickly turn into anger, you want to get revenge on the person, or you want to hurt them as they did to you. These are strong emotions to feel and can often be very challenging to ignore but remember that even if you did get the opportunity to enact your revenge, it probably won't help make you feel any better about the situation—it may even make you feel worse.

Once you find yourself in the grieving stage, you're going to feel sad at what you've lost—whether this is a close relationship, a physical thing, or an opportunity. When you get to this point, you will start to put yourself first and may consider the possibility of forgiving the person for what they did.

It's only after forgiving someone, or finding peace with a situation, that you can finally get to the healing stage and start fresh.

What's not forgiveness

Forgiveness is challenging. It involves facing your issues head-on and working to resolve your feelings and negative thoughts.

Forgiveness is not the following things:

- ☐ Ignoring the issue

- ☐ Rebounding e.g., getting into a new relationship, escaping your reality

☐ Pretending that your pain doesn't exist

☐ Picking up where you left off with your relationship

These things may be short-term solutions to help you feel some sense of normalcy, but the issue is still there—just brushed under the carpet.

You may initially feel better, but eventually you will have to face the consequences of the other person's actions. It may be triggered by a specific event, or something someone says, and all the emotions will come back again, sometimes even stronger after being ignored for so long.

To truly forgive someone, you must make a conscious choice to do so.

Forgiveness is not just for the benefit of the person that hurt you, it's most important for yourself. You're letting yourself let go of the anger and pain that a situation has caused you and allowing yourself to be at peace and move forward to the next stage in your life.

You can't spend your life with the weight of hurt on your back because it will eventually weigh you down. We've spoken about baggage earlier on in this book, and it's true that this baggage can cause many problems for you down the road if you don't stop and evaluate it.

Why should you forgive

There are many reasons why you should make the choice to forgive someone who wronged you in the past. Not only will it help bring closure to the relationship you have and allow you to process your feelings, but it can also help with the following things:

Improve other relationships

You can't form close, new relationships if you're still harboring anger and pain from previous ones.

If you have unresolved feelings against someone it may hold you back from getting the most out of new relationships. You might find yourself being unable to trust the new person or being unable to separate them from the person who caused you pain.

The new person in your life is not the same person as people from your past, you must remember that not all situations repeat themselves. You can't take your pain out on your new relationships because of how you've felt in the past as this will stop you from being able to create strong connections with people.

Improve your health

Anger and negative thoughts are bad for our health, they can cause a whole host of mental problems such as stress, anxiety and depression that can have a big impact on our daily lives.

By making the choice to forgive someone, we're also making the choice to release all our emotions and move forward with a lighter heart.

Opens new opportunities

When you're thinking negatively, it can be hard to envisage new opportunities for the future—even if they've been there all along.

Once you forgive and let go of the past, you will be able to look at life from a fresh perspective. You'll be able to identify new, positive opportunities and grasp them without worrying about anything holding you back.

It will make you happy in the long-term

Forgiveness helps you to heal and resolve your pain. The longer it takes for you to forgive, the longer it will take for your emotional wounds to heal.

The sooner you can forgive, the better, as oftentimes negative thoughts can seep into all aspects of your life when they are left to grow unchecked.

How to forgive

If you feel like you are ready to forgive, that's a great first step in your healing journey. Now it's come to the point where you must actually 'do the deed' and turn your thoughts into actions.

Here's how you can forgive someone from your past.

Talk through your feelings

To forgive, you must fully understand your feelings and emotions. The best way to do this is to talk them through with someone you trust, or a trained professional like a therapist.

Before talking, write down in a journal all the things that you want to cover. This way you can be sure that you're getting everything that you need to off your chest and that you're not leaving any feelings unresolved.

The feelings that you uncover in this conversation may be unwanted and painful to relive but you must not leave any emotional stone left unturned.

Break the pain down into sections and work on them one by one

Pain is a complex thing and cannot be resolved instantly. Start breaking down your feelings into sections and work on them one by one if it feels too overwhelming to go over it all in one go.

Communicate your forgiveness

Now's the time when you may need to talk to the person you're forgiving. Ask them if they're available to talk—in person is normally best, but if it can only be done through a phone call, you can make it work.

Tell them that you forgive them, make it clear what you are forgiving them for and explain why you have chosen to forgive them. This will give you closure and allow you to move on from the situation, whether that be with the person, or without them.

In some situations, it may not be possible to talk to the person. If this is the case, you can write them a letter where you discuss everything that you would in an in-person meeting. You don't even need to send the letter if you don't want to.

Alternatively, you can talk to someone you trust and tell them that you have chosen to forgive.

Forgive yourself

Another important aspect of forgiveness is learning to forgive yourself. In hard situations you may blame yourself or feel like you deserve the pain that you felt, but this is not true.

Self-compassion and self-forgiveness can often be complicated but may also be the things that are holding you back from being able to truly forgive.

The way that someone treats you is never a reflection of you, and it's never your fault.

CHAPTER 5 ACTIVITY

Ready to forgive someone, but don't know how to tell them? Here's a template for you to fill out that can be used when you decide to communicate your forgiveness— whether that be in-person or as a letter.

1. I wanted to talk to you today to let you know that I have decided to forgive you for.... *[Explain what they have done that needs forgiving]*

_____

_____

_____

2. Your actions made me feel… *[Explain the consequences of their actions and how it made you feel]*

_____

_____

_____

_____

_____

3. But today, I come to you with kindness and peace as I have overcome my feelings and decided to not let them affect me moving forward.

Over the past days/weeks/months/years I have learnt... *[Explain how you have concluded to forgive them and how you have come to understand the situation]*

_____

_____

_____

4. This situation caused me a lot of pain, but I know that I need to move on and to do that I must forgive you and let it go.

In the future, I hope that... *[What do you want in the future, do you want to talk to this person again? Do you want a relationship with them? Or do you just wish them well and plan to move on alone?]*

_____

_____

_____

Small daily habits to banish negative thoughts

B anishing negative thoughts is a marathon, not a sprint. It takes work to battle your past and move on to become a happier, more joyful person.

So far in this book, we have covered some deep topics that take a lot of energy and determination but will ultimately be the foundation blocks needed for you to build a happy life for yourself. It's also important to take each day at a time and focus on the small things that you can do as part of your daily routine to set yourself up for success.

In this chapter we'll be going over 10 simple daily habits that you can practice that will make your life much easier.

We're not suggesting you adopt all these habits, so feel free to pick and choose the ones that you think will fit in with your lifestyle. We're also not guaranteeing that all these habits will work for everyone—after all, we're all different and need different things to be happy.

1. Journaling

If you've never journaled before it can often be hard to pour all your thoughts and feeling onto a piece of paper. You may feel self-conscious and silly for being so open and honest with a notebook, but as you get used to it the practice becomes a lot easier.

Journaling is a good daily habit to adopt, and it's good to get into a routine where you journal for a certain amount of time and a particular time of the day, this way you encourage yourself to be thoughtful and intentional with your writing.

Your journal is your place to talk so it's completely up to you what you want to write about. Here are some prompts to help you get started. You can write about:

- ☐ How your day went

- ☐ How you felt throughout the day

- ☐ What you're looking forward to

- ☐ What was the most important part of your day?

- ☐ What's one thing that made you sad/happy during the day?

2. Meditation

If your negative thoughts leave you feeling stressed, anxious, or miserable, meditation is a good way to get in touch with your emotions and really delve deep into your feelings.

During meditation you're able to really focus on your feelings without distraction. The benefits of this mindfulness practice include being able to better understand your pain, lower stress levels, connect with your mind and body and stop distractions from impacting your flow.

If you've never meditated before, here's a quick guide on how you can do it effectively. You can also find guided meditation routines on YouTube or on meditation apps. In these routines, someone will talk you through what to do, what to think about and will help you feel at ease during what can be a very vulnerable experience.

- ☑ **Set a time limit:** How long do you want to meditate? For your first time you might want to start with a short timer of around 5 minutes so that you can get a feel for the process. As you become more experienced, you can start meditating for longer.

- ☑ **Take a seat:** Whether you want to sit on your bed, the floor or on a chair—it doesn't matter. Just make sure you're in a room where you feel calm and there isn't anything that could cause you a distraction.

☑ **Find a position that suits you:** You're going to be sitting down for a while, so make sure you're feeling comfortable. You may choose to sit on a chair with your feet on the floor, or cross-legged.

☑ **Close your eyes and connect with your body and breath:** Closing your eyes is optional but can be helpful to block out the world. Take time to feel and appreciate your body, focus on your breath and feel yourself start to calm down.

☑ **See where your mind takes you:** If you're doing a guided meditation, you may already have some questions that you want to think about, but it's also fine to go into meditation without anything in mind. Let your mind wander and see where it takes you.

☑ **Finish meditation:** Once your timer has gone off, slowly open your eyes or bring yourself back to the room you're in. Take time to embrace the emotions you're feeling and take stock of what you got out of your meditation session.

Meditation is a great skill to have, especially when you're trying to build a happier life for yourself as it gives you a chance to connect with yourself and think without having to worry about any of the other things that come with daily life.

3. Mantras

Mantras, or affirmations, are short phrases that you repeat to yourself that sets positive intentions for yourself. It may be something that you say, or write, every day to keep you on track to eliminate negative thinking or may be something that you say when you feel negative thoughts starting to creep their way into your head.

Here are some positive affirmations that you can use to eliminate unwanted thoughts:

- ☐ "I am the architect of my life; I built the foundations and I choose the contents"

- ☐ "The only moment that matters is the right here and right now"

- ☐ "Today I feel light and overflowing with happiness"

- ☐ "I rise above the negative thoughts that try to hold me back"

- ☐ "A river of compassion washes away all negative thoughts and replaces it with love"

☐ "I forgive those who hurt me in the past and I peacefully detach myself from all negative emotions"

☐ "Today I choose to abandon the habits that don't fill me with joy and work towards creating positive ones"

☐ "Though now may be challenging, it's only a short phase of my life and it shall pass"

4. Gratitude

We often spend so much of our time worrying or not appreciating the small things, so make sure that you take time each day to focus on gratitude.

There are so many things in life that you may have to feel grateful for, like:

☐ Your health

☐ Family and friends that love you

☐ A secure job

☐ Your courage and strength

☐ Your mind

☐ Your belongings and objects that strike joy in your heart

☐ The lessons that you have learnt throughout your life

As you go about your day, think of other things that you feel grateful for that you may not have noticed before. This could be like birds singing on your way to work, your morning coffee in your favorite café, your work colleague who always makes you laugh, or clear blue skies.

When you think about it, there really are a lot of things in life that fill us with gratitude and love.

5. Treat yourself

Take time to do indulge and treat yourself. This may have different meanings for different people and may involve giving yourself a 15-minute lay-in, cooking yourself a hearty breakfast instead of your normal cereal, getting a shot of vanilla syrup in your coffee, or buying yourself a new book to read.

Whatever it is that makes you feel special and treated, no matter how small it may be, make sure to take time to do it.

6. Set goals and ambitions

It's hard to dwell on the past and negative feelings when you're looking ahead. When you set yourself goals and think about your ambitions in life, you're giving yourself something that you can look forward to.

These goals don't have to be big and ground-breaking; they can be as simple as setting a goal to exercise once a week or learning a new dinner recipe, or as big as starting your own business or moving abroad.

Whatever it is, there's no better way to let go of the past than by focusing on all the great things you have coming your way in the future.

7. Self-care

Self-care has become a popular word that often gets confused with people being indulgent or selfish. This really isn't the case at all. Self-care means taking care of your mind and body so that you live each day to the fullest and feel healthy while doing it.

Self-care rituals can help you to deal with everyday stressors and, negative thoughts. It helps you to be the best person you can be and fulfill your full potential without holding yourself back.

To adopt self-care rituals in your daily life you can start with simple physical things like hygiene, nutrition and medical care that keeps your body fit and healthy. It can also include things like seeing your friends, taking a bath, or reading a self-help book—like this one!

Whatever it is that makes you feel relaxed and healthy, make time for it in your everyday life and you can call yourself a self-care expert.

8. Show up for the people around you

You know the feeling when you get a gift for someone, and they absolutely love it? It's a great feeling and is often much more enjoyable than simply buying a present for yourself.

Showing up and looking after the people around you is a great way to find joy every day. Not only can it distract you from the negative feelings in your life but can also help to give you purpose and a sense of satisfaction that you're doing something good for someone else.

Here are a few simple things that you can do daily to help the people around you:

☐ Buy your work colleague a coffee

☐ Compliment someone on what they're wearing

☐ Start up a conversation with the person you're sitting next to on the bus

☐ Call up a friend or family member and ask them how they are

☐ Buy your friend flowers or chocolate, just to show that you're thinking of them

☐   Invite someone out to dinner

☐   Clean your house and cook dinner for your partner

9. Find the silver linings

Instead of going about your day focusing on negative things, challenge yourself to find silver linings in even the most miserable of situations.

Once you start trying to find the positive in every situation, you'll instantly notice your mood start to improve and find that the situations that would often leave you feeling stressed or anxious, no longer bother you.

So, your car stopped working this morning, but it's a great opportunity to get some exercise and walk to work—you could even stop for a coffee on the way.

Your friend cancelled your plans to go out for dinner, but it means that you can get home early and spend time with your partner or use it as an opportunity to spend time on one of your hobbies.

You got some bad feedback on a piece of work you submitted to your boss, but everyone makes mistakes, and you now know exactly what you can do next time to make your work perfect.

See? Once you start looking for the silver linings in negative situations, they really don't seem so bad after all.

10. What sparks joy for you?

The final daily ritual that we recommend adopting to help eliminate negative thinking, let go of the past and find joy in your daily life is to find the thing that sparks joy for you.

Everyone has those things that make them feel happy; it could be taking your dog for a walk, going on a run, reading a book, or baking.

If you know what your 'thing' is, this is the secret to eliminating negative thoughts. Spend a little bit of time everyday doing things that make you feel truly joyful, that make you forget about the negative thoughts that constantly plague your brain.

CHAPTER 6 ACTIVITY

Another effective way to eliminate negative thinking is to set yourself routines that position yourself as a priority.

Having a routine that you follow gives you the chance to take control of your life and keep you focused on what's important—which isn't the negative thoughts.

Below you'll find a daily schedule, using a technique called time-blocking where you plan out your whole day by hour, start to think about everything you want to do and achieve tomorrow.

Date:	
8:00am	
9:00am	
10:00am	
11:00am	
12:00pm	
1:00pm	
2:00pm	

Date:	
3:00pm	
4:00pm	
5:00pm	
6:00pm	
7:00pm	
8:00pm	

The art of creating a fulfilling inner and outer environment

Happiness is not an end goal. It's something that needs to be constantly worked on and nurtured to lead a fulfilled life. Happiness is also not something that's just out there waiting for you to find it, you must choose it and embrace it for yourself.

Similarly, you can't rely on other people to bring you happiness. Sure, people may come who make you feel good and satisfied, but does it count as happiness if without them, you'd be left feeling sad and empty? We must be realistic with ourselves and understand that no one is going to come along and hand your happiness, served up on a silver plate, you must want it and find it within yourself.

Happiness starts by being cultivated from within. You can grow and nurture it within your inner environment, then allow it to radiate into all other aspects of your external life.

In this chapter we will be telling you how you can start creating a fulfilling inner and outer environment that helps you to focus on your own happiness.

What does happiness look like for you?

Happiness is not a commodity. It's not a physical thing that you can pick off the shelves in your local supermarket. Because of this, happiness looks completely different to different people.

Everyone has their own baseline when it comes to happiness. Some people may be naturally happier than others and have a much higher baseline that helps them to figure out if they're feeling happy or sad at any given moment.

Other people have a much lower baseline for happiness and may not even consider themselves a particularly happy person. This doesn't mean that they don't experience happiness in their life, it just means that happiness may not be their natural state of being.

Try to think about a moment in your life when you felt the happiest, or imagine the feeling of true happiness, what does it look like to you?

Come to terms with your own ideas of what happiness is and this will help you to set your intentions for cultivating a fulfilling inner and outer environment that will help you towards that place you're thinking of.

Happiness from the inside out

Although you may feel like you want to get started with surrounding yourself with things to make you happy, it's important to start with your inner self—you can worry about everything else later.

Here are some of the practices that you can adopt that will cultivate inner happiness.

Self-care

As we've mentioned in previous chapters, self-care can really work wonders for our mental health.

It's a chance for you to really put yourself first and focus on what makes you feel relaxed, happy and in control.

Making a conscious decision to prioritize your mental health is something that a lot of people want to do, but many simply don't because of the time you need to invest in it. However, no matter how much effort you need to put in, it will always be worth it

Redefine your outlook on life

Positive affirmations, looking for silver linings, and acknowledging when your brain is telling you lies are all important ways to redefine your outlook on life.

It is often a choice to be happy, just like it is a choice to decide to see the good in people and life. You can't always spend your life anticipating someone to come along and hurt you again or waiting for past mistakes to rear their heads again.

Sometimes you must put your trust in the process and believe that everything will be OK, and even if it's not, know that you are strong enough to be able to deal with whatever it may be.

Journaling

Putting pen to paper, or simply getting your thoughts and feelings off your chest through journaling is an excellent way to cultivate a positive inner environment.

No one should have to carry the load by themselves, and you'd be surprised at just how much a notebook is able to help you with managing the load.

Your journal won't judge you so you can feel free to say exactly how you feel, and sometimes seeing all your thoughts written out in front of you can make you feel completely different about them.

Learn to relinquish control

We must face it, although we all want to be in complete control of our lives, this isn't always the case.

Learning to relinquish control of the things that are out of your power is a good step to feeling freer and more lighthearted.

Just because you don't have control over a certain situation, doesn't mean that it's going to end badly for you, or anyone else. So, as The Beatles said, "Let it be".

Only worry about things that deserve your time

Like learning to relinquish control, it's also important to only reserve your mental capacity for things that really deserve your time.

It's not worth the stress and anxiety worrying about something that is out of your control or may not ever happen.

You should also not spend your time worrying about people and situations that aren't fulfilling to you. For example, if you have a friend that makes you feel bad and doesn't treat you well, you shouldn't spend your time worrying about them as they don't deserve your compassion.

Your outer environment reflects your inner self

Once you feel happy on the inside, it's time to shine and let all these positive feelings penetrate every other outer area of your life.

Here's how you can cultivate a happy outer environment:

Savor little joys

Happiness can come from anywhere, even the smallest things. Take time to be present in the moment and look out for the small things that make you feel happy; the smell of coffee, hearing the voice of a loved one on the phone, your bus arriving 1-minute early etc.

Once you slow down to savor the small, mundane things that make every day special, your overall mood will drastically start to improve.

Eliminate excess

One habit that we, as humans, have when we're feeling negative or low is thinking that we can buy our way out of sadness.

You can buy yourself new clothes, new gadgets, or any other physical object, but you quickly learn that these things don't make you happy. You may also find that having an excess of possessions can increase feelings of stress and negativity. Not only do they serve as a physical reminder of our low points, and attempts to get out of them, but can also make our space feel cluttered and full of unnecessary things.

Once you learn that excess doesn't equate to happiness, you'll realize that you don't really need much to make you happy.

Excess doesn't just apply to physical belongings, but also to how we manage our lives and time. There's no point constantly striving to do more, to work harder and do more things—in reality, less is more. Focus on the things that help you to reach your goals and eliminate all the other things that don't.

Surround yourself with things and people that spark joy

Following on from the previous point on excess, it's important to make sure that the things that you do choose to surround yourself with spark joy in you.

Take time to collect meaningful belongings that strike up a certain positive feeling in you. Whether that means investing in a good quality pair of shoes instead of 5 cheap pairs because they're comfortable, easy to walk in and will last you years and years or buying picture frames for your home where you can display photos of your nearest and dearest.

This approach also applies to people. The people in your life are there to help you on your journey and make you feel good while doing it—remember, that you should also be doing the same for them.

If there are people in your life that don't make you feel happy, or are causing you to feel sad and negative, these are not people you should be surrounding yourself with.

You should never feel bad for cutting people out of your life that don't deserve to be there. It's always better to have a small group of people around you that genuinely look out for you and care for you, compared to a large group of people that never seem to be there when you need them.

Spend money on experiences

After spending money on a new outfit, or decoration for your home, you probably feel satisfaction for a few minutes, that's until the novelty wears off and it just becomes another object in your house.

Physical objects don't bring about long-lasting satisfaction, this can only be achieved by experiences.

Your money is best spent on going on holiday, visiting new places, socializing with friends, or meeting new people. These are experiences that will enrich your life, help you to learn about yourself and others and teach you new things that you would have never known before.

These experiences also don't have to be large investments but are sure to create memories that will last you throughout your life. When it comes down to it, you probably won't remember the t-shirt you bought 20 years from now, but we're sure that you'll never forget a lifechanging trip to a new country with your best friends.

CHAPTER 7 ACTIVITY

Before going to bed, think about all the things that went well in your day and all the things that made you happy, then write it all down in your journal. This is known as 'gratitude journaling'.

Here are some common gratitude journal prompts to help get you started:

1. An accomplishment I'm proud of is…

2. A person that I'm happy to have in my life is…

3. Today I found comfort in…

4. My favorite moment of the day was…

5. The biggest gift in my life right now is…

6. Something beautiful I saw today that made me smile was…

7. My favorite part of my home is…

8. Today I am thankful for…

9. Some positive news I got recently is…

10. Today I showed gratitude for the people I love by…

Choosing relationships that serve you

As humans, we are social creatures that thrive off the relationships we have with other people, whether they be romantic, friendship or family relationships.

Even if you think that you're the most independent person in the world, you'll also find it hard to succeed without the help and support of the people who care about you.

When we build, strong positive relationships with other people we start to feel happier, more fulfilled and supported. However, if we put our energy into relationships that aren't fulfilling, the opposite can happen. We start to feel isolated, miserable—and ultimately let all those negative thoughts we try so hard to eliminate back into our heads again.

How to build positive relationships

Although relationships are so important to us as human beings, we are not all born with the natural ability to build these great relationships.

Relationships take hard work and patience, after all it can take time to build trust in another person.

Here are some of the things that you can practice that will make forming relationships much easier.

Be open and share

To build good relationships you must be open and willing to share parts of yourself with someone else—not all at once though!

It's hard to be friends with a closed book, if you don't share details of yourself the other person will never feel close to you, as they don't really know you.

Sure, there may be some things that you don't want to share with others—and that's OK, everyone has these things. But it is important to let other people in, tell them how you're feeling, share your plans and hobbies so that you can find common ground, keep conversations flowing and become closer.

Be consistent with your emotions

It's not great to be in a relationship of any kind with someone whose mood is constantly changing. If you find that your moods can sometimes be up and down, it can become stressful for the people around you as they never know what to expect from you.

When building relationships, we often must put aside our strong emotions so that we can be fully present with the other person and be able to engage with them without making our own emotions the priority.

Be a great listener

We all want to be around people who care about us and want to listen when we have something to say, and you should also be able to do the same for the people in your life.

When your friend, family member or partner comes to you to share something, you should make sure to really listen and try to understand their problem. We are all always so busy so once you start making time in your day to listen to the people around you, you'll quickly notice your relationships blooming.

Develop empathy

Empathy is your ability to really feel what someone else is feeling, it can take time to develop in a relationship but is often one of the main reasons why relationships can fail. If you don't develop empathy, you will never be able to fully understand the other person and their reasons for doing things.

To build a connection with another person you should be able to read them and relate to their emotions so that you can offer them support and develop mutual trust.

You know when you're speaking to a friend, and they know the exact right thing to say or do to make you feel better? It makes you feel great doesn't it, it shows you that this person really 'gets you'. This is an example of empathy in action and can make all the difference when trying to foster deep relationships.

Ask questions and be genuinely interested

Relationships are a 2-way street, we all want someone who's genuinely interested in us and asks us questions, and we should also do this for other people.

Especially when you meet a new person, asking the right questions is critical for building a solid foundation for a relationship to start. We can dig deeper into this person and learn more about them, once you show that you're trying to understand others, you'll notice them start to open and share even more with you.

Signs your relationship is positive

When you're looking to eliminate negative thinking in your life and find happiness, one of the things that could be holding you back from achieving this may not be yourself, it may be the people around you.

If you find yourself in relationships that aren't serving you, you may be feeling upset, self-conscious, and isolated. Although you may be feeling these emotions, sometimes it's not always clear when a relationship is truly toxic and not worth your energy.

It can also be especially hard to identify these toxic relationships when it's with someone that you've known for a long time, and your relationship has always been this way.

Think about the relationships that you have with your friends, partners, or family members—do you think that they are positive, and no it's not just about laughing and having things in common.

Here are some signs of a positive, healthy relationship:

☐   You trust each other

- ☐ You're able to speak your mind

- ☐ You can have your own space

- ☐ You can disagree and fight, but always make up and apologize

- ☐ You're realistic

- ☐ You both can make compromises

- ☐ You treat each other with kindness and respect

- ☐ You can talk to each other about anything

- ☐ You don't feel judged or belittled when you make mistakes

- ☐ You can let things go

What to do when a relationship isn't serving you

If you have looked through the list above and realized that a relationship you're in doesn't bring you any joy or happiness, you may choose to let this relationship go.

You should never feel bad for letting someone in your life go, no matter how long you've known them and regardless of all the good times you shared with each other in the past.

People change and relationships evolve, what worked 5 years ago is not guaranteed to work for the rest of your life. It can be a hard pill to swallow, but we also must accept that sometimes people aren't made to be in your life forever, sometimes they are just there to be in your life for a short period of time before you outgrow each other.

If it's time to let someone go, here are some things that you can do when a relationship isn't serving you.

Communicate your needs

Often you may not need to totally cut someone out of your life, it may just be a case of communicating your needs. The other person may have no idea that you're feeling sad in the relationship and may need to be told how you feel to decide that they can make changes to improve the situation.

For example, if you're in a romantic relationship and receiving words of affirmation is important to you, and you feel like you don't get that from your partner. This may not be their default way of showing affection and they may not even realize that this is an important thing for you.

If you're able to explain to them why you feel sad and why words of affirmation are important to you, they will start to understand how you feel and make a conscious effort to show this to you.

The first step is always talking to the other person as you could find a resolution that you may not have known was an option. You may also find from this discussion that the person is unable to compromise or unable to give you what you need. This is a sign that the relationship has run its course and is at an end.

It's normally best to tell someone when you think a relationship has ended. Sometimes things naturally end, and nothing needs to be said, but we should always let the other person know that things aren't working rather than just moving on alone.

Forgive

Sometimes relationships don't come to a mutual end, or relationships are forced to end because of the actions of one of the people.

When these kinds of closes come about you may have to practice forgiveness. We went through how to do this in an early chapter, but it's an important step in moving on and becoming better at relationships in the future.

You must process the relationship, accept what happened and find closure and peace for yourself, which can often only be done by forgiving the other person for what they did to you.

Reconnect with yourself

Because relationships are such an important part of who we are, when one ends, we may start to feel lost without that other person around.

In these situations, it's best to reconnect with yourself. What do you enjoy doing? What do you want out of future relationships?

Start to live for yourself, focus on what you consider most important. These are the things that are going to give you the ability to form better, stronger relationships in the future.

CHAPTER 8 ACTIVITY

Below you'll find an outline of the human body which represents your perfect person. Think about all the qualities that you would look for in a relationship (friendship, family or romantic) and write them down around the outline.

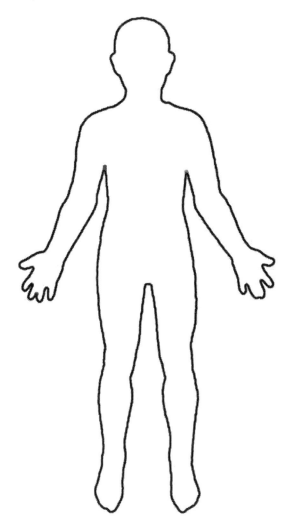

How to find motivation amongst the chaos

You may sometimes feel that life is hard, and things never seem to go your way, this can leave you feeling demotivated and reinforces the negative thinking that we have been trying to eliminate.

Life can also be chaotic, unplanned, and messy and although it can be easy to stay calm when things are going your way, it's much harder to try and be positive when things are a bit crazy.

Things aren't always going to go your way, that's not how life works. You don't have much of a choice about many things, but what you can do is choose how you react to them.

No matter how hard things seem at the time, there are always plenty of ways that you can find motivation and peace in the chaos.

The next time you start to feel overwhelmed, stressed, or simply feeling that life is getting to you, here are some things that you can do to eliminate negative thinking and start finding motivation and joy in your everyday again.

Put yourself first

When you're busy and stressed it can be easy to let yourself go. You may have a huge deadline coming up at work so you start staying up later, ordering takeaway, stop exercising just so that you can get everything completed.

Behaving like this may help you hit the deadline eventually, but in the meantime, you are sabotaging yourself and putting yourself on the right track to burn out. When life starts getting hard, you must not forget about what's most important—your health and happiness.

Healthy bodies and minds are key to our survival, and we must make sure that we're being kind to ourselves to achieve these things. Sure, it can be easy to let ourselves go, and it might feel rewarding to hit a deadline, but what is the price that you've paid for it? If it means your body feels rubbish because you haven't been fueling it properly, or that you feel self-conscious about your appearance after not treating yourself well, is hitting the deadline worth it?

Keep focused on your goals

In tough times it can be hard to look to the future and work towards our goals, as so much of our attention is focused on getting through daily life.

When you lose sight of your goals and ambitions, it can be hard to pick yourself up and find motivation as you have nothing to look forward to and work towards.

If you find your attention straying from your future, consider writing down your goals on a piece of paper and sticking them on the wall behind your desk, in your kitchen or anywhere in your room that you look at frequently. Having your goals written down will be a constant reminder of what you're doing everything for, where you want to be and why you're working hard at the moment.

There are people that care

You may find that when you feel demotivated you completely shut down, you start ignoring text messages, forget to reach out to your friends and avoid socializing.

Remember that you are surrounded by people who care about you and who want to listen and support you—you just must let them do this.

If you're feeling demotivated, take the time to call a friend. You can either discuss how you're feeling, and they can offer advice and motivate you that everything's going to be OK, or you can simply talk about anything to distract yourself from your situation.

Open your mind to new opportunities

If you feel like there's no way out of your current stressful situation, it may be that they are there, but you're just not open to embracing them.

Once you start to open your mind, new opportunities will seem to come out of nowhere. These opportunities may be the answer to all your current issues or be the solution to help you get up and motivated.

Learn how to adapt

We're creatures of habit that always seem to react to situations in the same way repeatedly, even when we know that our behavior never achieves the outcome we want.

Next time something demotivating happens to you, try and act differently and adapt to the situation. For example, if you get bad feedback at work, you may normally be upset and feel down, instead why don't you adapt and ask your manager what you can do better?

CHAPTER 9 ACTIVITY

Everyone has different ways of motivating themselves and different things that can help them to get out of bed in the morning—these are our personal motivators, what are yours?

Below you'll find a table that shows some of the most common personal motivators. Go through each one and circle the ones that you relate to. We've also included some blank spaces in the table where you can write any motivators that we didn't cover!

Power	Love	Money	Success
Influence	Achievement	Family	Friends
Fulfilment	Intelligence	Freedom	Sex
Recognition	Reward	Personal Growth	Honor
Status	Self-validation	Desire to be the best	Passion
The future	Promotion	Security	Control

Tactics to pick yourself up when you regress

Healing and learning to forgive, let go of the past and move on is not a linear journey. There's no straight path to reach your intended goal, your path to success will be up and down and may involve periods of time when you regress into your old habits.

Whatever your path to success looks like—it's OK. There's no right or wrong way to change your life and become a happier person. This journey looks completely different for every single person.

When you first feel signs of regression in your journey, it can be easy to give up and think that you're never going to be able to get back onto the path. But remember that the only thing that will stop you from achieving your goal are thoughts like these.

There are plenty of ways that you can pick yourself up when you're not doing your best, and regression doesn't mean that your journey is impossible and unreachable.

Here are some tactics that you can use to pick yourself up when you regress emotionally.

Remind yourself why you are doing this

Everyone has their own personal reasons for wanting to improve their lives and let go of the past—what are yours?

Think about the reasons you decided to start this journey. Is it so that you can eliminate negative thinking, let go of past experiences that are holding you back, learn to forgive someone who hurt you in the past, or so that you can wake up every day happy and grateful for your life?

Whatever your reason may be for going on this emotional journey, focus on that and it will help you to pick yourself back up and continue with your healing process.

Look at how far you've come

When you regress it can be hard to see just how far you've come from the place that you started. Although you may have moved back slightly, you're not starting at the beginning all over again.

Maybe you've been able to understand why someone hurt you, or you've been able to communicate your needs with a friend or family member so that you can start the process of being happier.

Whatever it is that you've done, you're not the same person as you were at the start anymore and be proud of that! You've already achieved so much, so sure you may not be at the exact point that you want to be at right now, but you're still learning and improving every day and you're not going to let yourself get in the way of that.

Ask yourself how you feel

Your feelings are important and take time to really ask yourself how you feel about this regression. You may be feeling disappointed, stressed, or anxious about the fact that you weren't able to stay on track.

Take time to write your feelings down, or simply sit down and think about them and understand what they mean. These feelings will often be hard to recognize and unwanted, but really allowing yourself to feel them is the only way that you'll be able to move forward. It will also serve as a reminder in the future to keep on track, so you don't have to experience these emotions again.

Fake it until you make it

Sometimes the best thing to do is to just respond to situations in a way that don't exactly align with how you're feeling. If you're feeling sad, try to do things that make you feel happy or think positive thoughts, after doing this for a while you'll start to realize that these 'fake happy' feelings have become real.

No one knows what's going on inside of your head apart from you, how are they supposed to know that you're feeling disappointed and sad on the inside?

We of course don't want you to suppress your emotions as this can cause negative effects, but sometimes it can feel good to not give negative thinking power over you and instead make up for them by being extra happy and positive.

Seek support

You never have to feel like you're going through something on your own, and don't try to close yourself off when you're feeling down and miserable.

It's important to reach out and seek support from the people around us when we are going through a hard time, no one wants to see you try and battle everything on your own.

If you've regressed emotionally and are falling victim to negative thoughts again, schedule a coffee date with a friend, or give your parents a call to tell them that you're not doing well and could use some advice or support.

Think about how you would feel if you knew that someone close to you was going through a hard time, you'd want to do whatever you could to make them feel better again, right? We're sure that your loved ones also want to do the same for you.

We wouldn't be anything without the support from those around us, and they can be the answer to finding motivation and picking yourself up again when you've faced an emotional setback.

Conclusion & resources

We've come to the end of this book now, and we hope that you have found something in these pages that will help you to be happy and forgive.

We know that the past can often be a burden and hold us back from achieving what we all really want—true happiness and peace. But by going through the contents of this book and putting into practice some of our suggestions, we are positive that soon you'll be able to find the joy in the every day again.

Everyone can change their own life and want something better for themselves, but not everyone has the motivation and determination to put the work in to make the change.

We will end this book as we started it, by reminding you that no matter what you may think, **you are not your past.**

Of course, your past can often be part of what makes you, you, but it does not define the person that you have become and should not hold you back from being the person that you want to be. Everyone changes so much in their life, the person that you were yesterday is not the person that you have become today, so don't let the past versions of yourself affect you in the present.

Similarly, we are not defined by our thoughts. Our thoughts can sometimes lie to us and make us feel demotivated and sad, but it's a choice whether you give them the power to do this.

Choosing to let go of the past is a personal decision, and there's never a right or wrong time to decide to do this. By reading this book, you have made the first step of your journey, and everything that comes after this will become easier and easier as you travel along.

Or, if you've read this book and decided that you don't feel ready to let go of the past *just yet* that's also OK. Your journey to happiness is exactly that—yours and it's not for anyone else to say when you should set off on this journey.

This book has given you a mix of scientific insights, guides and activities that have helped to focus your mind on how to enjoy the everyday, and tips on how you can eliminate negative thinking in your life for good. This book should empower you to grab onto your life with both hands on the steering wheel and make a positive difference.

Our closing words to this book, as we bid farewell is to give you 4 quick things that you can do *right now* to continue the learnings that you started in this book, we hope they set you up for success.

1. Look through your activities

At the end of almost every chapter in this book we asked you to complete an activity. Have a look through your work and reflect on what you wrote down, how it made you feel.

Then imagine yourself in a year's time, do you think you will complete these activities differently? What do you think of this new person that's coming back to this book again?

2. Read the introduction again

It might feel like a long time since you read the introduction of this book, since reading it you've learnt a lot and your outlook on happiness has probably changed.

Revisit the introduction and read it again, thinking about all the knowledge you've acquired since you first laid eyes on it. What does it mean to you now? Have your thoughts and feelings changed?

3. Check out at least one of the resources that we've mentioned below

Although we think this book is a great resource for people who want to eliminate negative thinking, we're also going to include a list of other resources that you can use to continue learning.

Pick one, or however many you'd like, of the resources below and read, watch, or listen to it. How do the opinions of this resource differ from what you learnt in this book? Do their teachings on happiness resonate with you more, or less than our book did?

4. Call a friend

Our final tip is to get on your phone and call a friend or family member! We've spoken a lot in this book about the importance of the people around you and how they can help in your journey, so put the effort in to reach out to them and let them into your head.

Resources

Your journey to move on from the past and be happier doesn't finish the second you close this book, it's only the start of great things to come for you.

Happiness is like a plant that needs constant, water, care, and attention for it to bloom into something beautiful. You should adopt a similar approach by making small improvements in your life every day and putting the work in to become a happier individual.

Below, we've collated a list of some of the best happiness-boosting resources that can help you to find joy in everyday life and continue to take steps on your happiness journey.

You'll find all the best books to read, podcasts to listen to and documentaries to watch that will give you the daily boost of motivation you need to live intentionally and happily.

Books to read

- ☐ The Art of Happiness – the Dalai Lama and Howard C. Cutler

- ☐ Happiness Is an Inside Job: Practicing for a Joyful Life – Sylvia Boorstein

- ☐ Getting Back to Happy: Change Your Thoughts, Change Your Reality, and Turn Your Trials into Triumphs – Angel Chernoff and Marc Chernoff

- ☐ The Power – Rhonda Byrne

- ☐ The Power of Now – Eckhart Toll

Documentaries to watch

- ☐ Minimalism: A Documentary About the Important Things

- ☐ I Am

- ☐ Footprints: The Path of Your Life

- ☐ Tony Robbins: I Am not Your Guru

- ☐ Project Happiness

Podcasts to listen to

- ☐ 10% Happier with Dan Harris

- ☐ Happier with Gretchen Rubin

- ☐ The Good Life Project

- ☐ The Science of Happiness

- ☐ The Tim Ferriss Show

Websites to visit

- ☐ Calm.com

- ☐ Happier.com

- ☐ GretchenRubin.com

- ☐ Zenhabits.net

- ☐ Tinybuddha.com

Disclaimer

This book contains opinions and ideas of the author and is meant to teach the reader informative and helpful knowledge while due care should be taken by the user in the application of the information provided. The instructions and strategies are possibly not right for every reader and there is no guarantee that they work for everyone. Using this book and implementing the information/recipes therein contained is explicitly your own responsibility and risk. This work with all its contents, does not guarantee correctness, completion, quality or correctness of the provided information. Misinformation or misprints cannot be completely eliminated.

Printed in Great Britain
by Amazon